Prayerful

Passages

Asking God's Help in Reconciliation,
Separation, and Divorce

Jack H. Emmott

DENVER, COLORADO

For my wife, Dorothy, and my mother, Lucile,
for through them,
I have seen and received the Love of God.

What others are saying about *Prayerful Passages* ...

When we are faced with the daunting prospect of marital conflict, separation, or divorce, we often cannot find the words to express our deepest thoughts and feelings. Jack Emmott's *Prayerful Passages* gives us the words we need—words that can open our hearts to the guidance and healing that is available through the grace of God. For those who are seeking reconciliation and those who are dealing with the loss of their marriage, these prayers will impart comfort and hope.

Gregory Schaefer, Ph.D.
Clinical Psychologist

Going through my divorce was the hardest thing I've ever done. As a Christian, I struggled to find prayers to express what I felt. This book, *Prayerful Passages,* captures many of the difficult feelings I had and still have. This book helps me cry out to God in prayer rather than just wrestling with my feelings alone. I believe that God has blessed Jack Emmott, and that these blessings will continue to shower in the lives this book touches.

John D. Glaze
Divorce Client

A compelling sharing of compassion—this book shows the impact a prayerful, Christ-centered life can have on the human spirit. What a powerful read . . . I was wowed by its wisdom.

Larry R. Cook, CPA
Financial Advisor

Whether you are clergy, a counselor, or a spouse, *Prayerful Passages* guides you through each step of asking for God's help in reconciliation, separation, and divorce.

Dr. Mary Anne Knolle, LFMT, LC

Through this simple book of prayers, Jack Emmott speaks personally, knowledgeably and soulfully to those who are facing crises in marriage, separation, or divorce. His thought-provoking prayers provide very practical and prayerful insights that help to encourage couples to sustain their commitment to marriage, or, if that is not possible, to honor and respect each other in future proceedings. The author's wisdom and faith shine through the pages.

Mary Kay Kickels, Ed.D.
Consultant, Higher Education

Whether you are trying to save your marriage or are facing divorce, the prayers to create your peaceful future lie within these pages.

Tracy Stewart, CPA
Financial Advisor

All you have to do is open to the table of contents to see the brilliance of this wise voice that pushes us all to see the world as a more inclusive, loving place where we are all perfectly imperfect children of God. Jack offers his reader empathy, wisdom and redemption for the human spirit. Don't miss the wisdom of a man who has lived into surrender at an early age as his polio left him trapped in an iron lung to survive. But, he didn't just survive; he blossomed and thrives today, venerating the love of the Divine for all of us. This is a must-read for all of us who want to live more fully into our loving relationships.

Micki Grimland, LCSW
Owner and Chief Psychotherapist
Southwest Psychotherapy Associates
(As seen on *Oprah* and *Great Day Houston*)

Life, for all of us, is filled with challenges. Many people need and want spiritual guidance during this time, but don't know where, or how, to begin. This book offers many prayers, specific to the concern, for those who can't seem to find their own words. Thank you, Jack, for your insight and wisdom shared in this book.

Linda Solomon
Marriage and Family Therapist

Table of Contents

Chapter Three: Prayers During Separation

Chapter Four: Prayers During Divorce

Chapter Five: Prayers for After the Divorce

Chapter Six: Universal Prayers During Reconciliation/Separation/Divorce

Chapter Seven: My Prayers for God's Help

Acknowledgements

Prayerful Passages was born out of the quietude of prayer. Long it has been said there are no mere coincidences in following a Holy or spiritual path. If this little book of prayers has wings and does great things in God's Kingdom on Earth, it is because God sent to me beautifully gifted, talented souls. Without their God-given gifts, *Prayerful Passages* would never have been published. I give thanks to God for my editor Sarah Cortez, poet, mentor and friend whose art and discernment enhanced the strength and clarity of this work. To my publicist Ann Boland who is encourager and insightful spreader of the good news about my book. To Carol Wilhelm and Maureen Doherty, my intellectual property lawyers who both gave me so much more than just legal advice. To my brother-inventor-printer-entrepreneur Gary Emmott and graphic artist Helen Mahnke for because of them I know that the reader can tell a book by its cover. To my cousin Allison Dawson for typing the never-ending drafts of the pages of this book. To Justin Romack my webmaster who is totally blind but sees more with his creative heart than a person with 20/20 vision. To my wife Dorothy for affording me the solitude I needed to focus on writing and critical constructive advice on the work.

Thanks be to God and to these wondrous souls for giving life to this work and their love to me.

ONE

What I Believe

I BELIEVE IN marriage. Through the grace of God, I am married to an angel, Dorothy, my best friend and true love of over forty years. I know the hard work and deep love it takes to have a happy, successful marriage. I can undeniably say that prayer has helped both of us in our marriage.

As a family law attorney for decades and faithful Christian my entire life, I also believe that divorce can be a matter of last resort if a Christian couple cannot save a marriage through pastoral care, marriage counseling, and the help of God obtained through prayer.

Divorce is a crisis. In my law practice, I have helped hundreds of Christian couples navigate the labyrinth of the legal process related to divorce. I have observed that couples who have strong anchors in a chosen faith and prayer life seem more likely to reconcile, or do what needs to be done to save the marriage. And those couples, who do not reconcile, consistently do better during divorce, during the transition from one house to two separate loving homes, and in sharing their children rather than dividing them like property.

You might ask how I learned about the power of prayer and God's presence. Let me tell you a little of my story.

At the age of six, I was paralyzed from the neck down by polio. I lay in a hospital bed. Quarantined, unable to move a toe or finger. Separated from those I loved: Mommy, Daddy, sister Carolyn, brother Charles.

I felt completely powerless and alone. Yet I knew my loving God had not abandoned me. He could always be summoned in prayer to be with me in my pain.

You see, through my devoted mother Lucile, God had already given me the gift of the power of prayer. Before the onset of polio for as long as I could remember, every night Mother had us kneel beside her at bedtime and say the words of the *Lord's Prayer* in unison with her. It had been a comfort and ritual at home when I was full of health and strength. Now, it became a comfort and ritual at Hedgecroft Hospital when I was frightened, alone, and weak. Even though I could no longer kneel, I was still able to pray.

As a dutiful six-year-old boy, I said the *Lord's Prayer* every day at Hedgecroft Hospital for the better part of a year. After the initial onset of polio and partial recovery from paralysis, there were many other Biblical journeys for me: operations on my feet, right leg and both hands, three steel rods inserted in my back to keep my spine from further scoliosis, broken bones, accidents, post-polio syndrome, five years in the iron lung, three floods in our beloved home.

Yet my faith in God, the presence of His angels bending over me, and the power of prayer unfailingly saw me through those trials and many others.

I believe God listens to every prayer from me and from every one of His children.

In prayer, we get clarity from God's lips as to what we need to do or not do in relation to Him, to ourselves, and to those around us, including our spouses and children. In trying to save a marriage in crisis and in the midst of divorce, the emotion and sense of loss are so profound that clarity is not possible or, at least, is in very short supply.

We obtain clarity through the gift of discernment which requires fully listening with the "ear of one's heart" (to quote St. Benedict) in the quietude of prayer. In that silent, bountiful place, God exclaims, "Pray to Me, my child, and the answers shall certainly come."

Indeed, God has a purpose which He conceived for each of us before our births. Our spiritual journey is to know, discover, and live that purpose for ourselves and, most importantly, for others. Thus, we honor and give praise to God for the gift of life. And, no, life is *not* fair. It is simply a blessing.

I believe one of the purposes for which God created me was to survive polio, to learn difficult lessons in the darkness of despair, and to become a Christian family law attorney and author.

These are some of the questions I have pondered deeply and talked to God about in prayer:

- Can I be used as an instrument of reconciliation to save marriages?
- Can I encourage spouses to separate and use prayer for clarity and for reconciliation?

- Where is God for each spouse and his/her children?

- What part can prayer play in preserving the sacrament of marriage for the husband and wife?

- How can daily prayer help spouses transition from married to single life in a more loving, less hurtful, and healthier way?

- How might prayer help the divorcing parents be better at co-parenting their children both during and after the divorce?

- What different kind of legacy is left for children by parents who pray daily seeking Godly answers?

- Can the power of prayer be used by parents to safeguard their children from harm?

In prayer, I heard a voice say: "Write a book called *Prayerful Passages*." God helped me envision writing a comforting resource for married couples in their quest to preserve their marriage or lessen the harm done in divorce.

As I continued to pray and listen more deeply to God, the words for these prayers began flowing. The words were put on paper. Prayers to save a marriage. Prayers to know what to do. Prayers for what to say to a spouse and children. Prayers for direction. Prayers for strength. Prayers to feel a Divine Presence in the darkness. Prayers for forgiveness. Prayers to heal a broken heart. And so many more.

The prayers I have written with God's help are only examples. If you wish, create the words for your own prayers. What is important is that you spend time alone with God.

May God bless you in every difficult and troubling journey or prayerful passage in your life. May you remember that Earthly challenges come and go. But, in prayer, may you learn that God's love for you is forever through the Almighty Father, in the name of His Son Jesus Christ, the Savior of all humankind and the Prince of Peace. Amen.

TWO

Prayers for Reconciliation

Prayer for Assistance in Time of Struggle for Reconciliation

Almighty God, as I struggle to honor my marriage vows to my spouse and my covenant with You, please use me as Your instrument to do Your will. Fill me, as Your vessel, with Your infinite love and grace so that I may better love my spouse and reflect Your healing light on our broken relationship as man and wife.

In the name of Your Son Jesus Christ, may You also bestow the same love and light on my spouse as You will on me, so that we may share the blessing of marriage until death do us part. Amen.

Prayer for Peace

Almighty God, I am emotionally and physically ill because of the unhealthy, stressful relationship I have with my spouse. I am so upset and anxious I have difficulty sleeping, or I worry too much, fearing that divorce is inevitable.

As I work to save our marriage, please help me have faith in You and avoid unnecessary conflict. Show me how to solve our marital problems outside the presence of our child/children.

Heavenly Father, I ask that You answer my prayers for peace, in the name of your Son Jesus Christ, the Prince of Peace. Amen.

Prayer for Pastoral Care

Almighty God, I desperately need the support and guidance of a minister. I have learned that I cannot save our marriage by myself. Please help me find a minister, pastor, or priest who is best suited to meet our needs. Through such pastoral care, may I receive guidance and wisdom. Help me learn the ways our marriage can be saved, and then blossom in the light of Your love for us. Amen.

Prayer for Marriage Counseling

Almighty God, we cannot save our marriage without help from others. Please help me and my spouse find a Christian marriage counselor who is best suited to meet our needs. May our counselor help us listen in a deep way, so we each can hear the other with new understanding and compassion. Help us speak truthfully but not hurtfully, so we can each be heard with wisdom by the other.

Heavenly Father, please give me the strength and openness to make full use of the tools and coping skills I learn from our marriage counselor. Thank You for the help and guidance You have already sent us. Amen.

Prayer to be Open to Forgiveness and to Be Forgiven

Almighty God, I am so angry and hurt because my spouse has betrayed my trust. Despite the heartbreaking betrayal, my spouse has asked me for forgiveness to be able to save our marriage.

Heavenly Father, please open my heart to hope and healing. Although I find myself blaming my spouse for all of our marriage problems, I realize that what I have done or not done may be part of the problem. Please help me recognize and take responsibility for my part in our problems.

Each of us has a share in the breakup of our marriage. Both of us have a part to play in its reconciliation. Please help each of us forgive the other, as You forgive those who accept Christ as Lord and ask for Your forgiveness. Amen.

Prayer for Forgiveness

Almighty God, I am having great difficulty opening up my heart to save our marriage because my spouse has become addicted to (alcohol/drugs/pornography). I do not know how to overcome these intense feelings. My spouse wants to save our marriage. So, he/she has sought treatment and promises to work a 12-step program.

God, please help me know that my spouse is ill. Help me find compassion and understanding for the addiction which has threatened our marriage. I pray that You open my heart to hope and healing, so that I may do my part to save the marriage. Please shower Your loving presence and grace upon my spouse so that he/she maintains sobriety and faith in You. Amen.

Prayer for Help with Addiction

Almighty God, I confess that I have a problem with addiction that has caused my marriage to suffer. Please forgive me for what I have not done to overcome my destructive addiction.

I pray today that You will forgive me for my sins and offer me Your devoted love and support. In the darkness of addiction, please shine the Light of Christ upon me. In Your Holy Grace, lift me out of this despairing place, so that I can face and overcome my addiction and be sober again for those I love and those who love me. Amen.

Prayer for Forgiveness from God

Almighty God, I have sinned against You. I have broken our marriage vow to be faithful to my spouse. I am truly sorry and ask for Your forgiveness. I pray that, in time, my spouse can forgive me too and be willing to continue to work on saving our marriage.

Please help me to be faithful to You and to my spouse. In the name of Your Son Jesus Christ, whose death took away the sins of the world, I pray that You grant me forgiveness, as I am truly repentant. Amen.

Prayer for Answers

Almighty God, in Holy Scripture, and in the life, death, and resurrection of Your Son Jesus Christ, You have revealed Your plan for humankind. Through faith, I know You have a plan and purpose for me in facing this crisis in my marriage. As I say my daily prayers, help me feel Your presence. From Your Heavenly Presence, please let me hear the answers I need to save the marriage. Amen.

Prayer to Feel, Express and Share Joy

Almighty Father, I give thanks to You for the Christian counseling my spouse and I are receiving at this time. For years, I have felt no hope or joy to share with my spouse or to show to our child/children. With prayer and counseling, I have begun to feel the warmth of the glowing ember of renewed love in my heart. I pray that laughter will once again be heard in our household and that our child/children can see honest signs of love and affection between us. Amen.

Prayer for Support

Almighty God, Your Son, Our Savior, did not die alone on the cross at Calvary. You did not abandon Him, but rather lifted Him in triumph as Eternal

Savior of the World. I pray for Your support as I agonize and struggle to preserve our marriage.

In prayer, please remind me that in my suffering, like Jesus, I am not alone. You, Your Son, and Your angels are with me always. Amen.

Prayer to Make Room for the Still, Quiet Place

Almighty God, my head is spinning. At night, when I should be sleeping, my mind is awake. I worry that the stress will cause me to become seriously ill. God, please help me find that still quiet, peaceful place I knew as a child with sand between my toes at the beach. A place where all my worldly needs were met by my mother and father, and when my only spiritual needs were to love You and be loved by You, then to be with You at church and in prayer.

Now, as an adult, I yearn for that same quiet place. Help me to find Your Holy Presence, so I might become the spouse, parent, and believer that You intend for me to become. Amen.

Prayer for God's Guidance on the Path to Reconciliation

Heavenly Father, my heart is heavy because my marriage is in grave trouble. I feel lost and alone. I do not know where to go or who to turn to for help besides You. In Your mercy, please show me that I am not alone and that You are with me. I do not want to divorce. I do not want to break my marriage vows to my spouse or to break my covenant with You, after You blessed us with the Holy sacrament of marriage.

As I pray in the darkness and seek guidance from You, please illuminate the path before me. Please show us the way to save our marriage and how to love one another until death do us part. Amen.

Prayer to Explore All Options to Save the Marriage

Almighty Father, I pray that You will reveal to me in prayer, in marriage counseling, and in the voices of Your angels, all the ways to save my marriage. If divorce comes to pass, may that passage be taken only after my spouse and I have totally explored all options in good faith to try to save the marriage.

I thank you, Heavenly Father, for the abundance of grace and guidance you have already sent to us. Amen.

Prayer for a Miracle to Save Our Marriage

Heavenly Father, I have struggled and prayed to save our marriage. Despite all my efforts, despite pastoral care, marriage counseling and prayer, our marriage seems doomed and without hope for reconciliation.

In You, I know all things are possible. At Cana, You turned water into wine. You fed 5,000 people bountifully with a few loaves and fishes in a deserted place. If it be Your will, I ask that You miraculously save our marriage. In You, I have faith that the impossible can be made possible. Hopelessness can give way to hope. I ask for Your miraculous healing of our broken marriage and our wounded hearts. Amen.

THREE

Prayers During Separation

Prayer at Time of Separation

Almighty God, today we are separating. I will be moving out of the home we have lived in as a "whole" family. When I move out, please help me to remain calm. It will not do any good for me, my spouse, or our child/children to witness tears, drama, or resentful looks when I leave. I pray that leaving is the first step in a process to work on our marital issues separately.

I also pray that, in separation, with Your help, we will find our way back to one another and preserve the union of two You intended to be one in marriage through Your Holy Grace. Amen.

Prayer During a Trial Separation

Almighty God, I have told my spouse I do not want a divorce, but it is hard to find clarity and direction for what to do to repair our marriage while we live under the same roof. My spouse and I have agreed to a trial separation.

While we are separated, Heavenly Father, please help us salvage our marriage. I pray that our time apart, while still working with a Christian marriage counselor, will reunite us and save our marriage. I believe that reconciliation honors our covenant with You and will renew our vows of love, trust, and loyalty to one another. Amen.

Prayer for Discernment in Separation

Almighty God, despite our efforts to remain in the same household working on our marriage, we feel we need to live separately from one another at this time.

I pray that our separation is only temporary. As Your Son Jesus went to the mountainside to pray and be alone with You, may we both use this separation to be with You in prayer. Please send us the grace to make room in our hearts for each other, to feel Your presence through prayer, and to receive the daily blessing of discernment, so that we may continue to be the husband and wife that You intended on our wedding day. Amen.

Prayer for Spiritual Watchfulness

Almighty God, Your Kingdom has no boundaries. Through Your Son Jesus Christ, and the intercession of Your saints, angels, and archangels, we have been shown the way to Heaven. As I move through each day during our trial separation, may I be ever watchful for the signs that You are near me. May I see Your angels, who are Your messengers in my midst, bending over me. May I hear in my heart the messages You send me.

Heavenly Father, help me to discern the way to reconcile with my spouse, to live more richly, to love more deeply, to live and die more devoted to You, and to be more deserving of admittance into Your Heavenly Kingdom. Amen

Prayer for Flexibility During Separation

Almighty God, I pray that You will give my spouse and I the courage and strength to try all things to save our marriage while we are separated. If divorce happens, I never want to ask myself if I have tried everything I knew to save our marriage. Amen.

Prayer to Separate from an Abusive Spouse

Almighty God, I have been with my abusive spouse so long that I cannot see clearly how to separate and spare myself and our child/children from further conflict, violence, and pain. I have lived so long with abuse that I do not know the difference between the darkness and the light, or between love and hate.

Heavenly Father, please give me the strength and courage to separate. Please empower my spouse to surrender his/her anger and abusiveness to You, so that one day we may be able to safely live and love one another in the same house. In the future, please help our child/children not create a home with the kind of abuse they experienced in childhood with us. Amen.

Prayer for Protection from Harm and Abuse

Almighty Father, my spouse has physically abused me. I am rightfully afraid of further abuse and harm. As I hope for reconciliation or a safe separation from my spouse and seek to protect the child/children and myself from further abuse, I pray that You shield us with Your armor of Light.

I pray that You shine the Light of Christ Jesus on the darkness of evil and anger in my spouse. May You cast out the demons of anger from my spouse and cure that which is ill, while You care for us in this difficult journey. Amen.

Prayer for God to Transform the Bad into Good

Almighty Father, I have made such a mess of things. I have let down my spouse and our child/ children. I have hurt them through my acts and deeds. I have sinned against You.

The stories in the Bible from Jacob to Jonah and the Whale demonstrate how You and Your Love transform even bad into good. In prayer and in my pleas for forgiveness, please take the mess I have made and turn it into good for my spouse, our child/children, and our Christian family. Amen.

Prayer for Thankfulness

Almighty Father, in separation I find myself in a dark and dreary place. I am obsessing on all that I have lost or may lose if my marriage to my spouse is not saved. In my daily prayer, please help me step out of the darkness and into Your Holy Light. With You, may my heart be evermore thankful for the gifts of love I have received from You, from Your Son Jesus, the Risen Christ, and Your angels on Earth and in Heaven. Amen.

Prayer to Live Close to My Spouse During Separation

Almighty God, I feel so angry at my spouse that I want to live as far from him/her as possible during our separation. However, I have learned from our Christian counselor that our child/children will benefit in many ways if we live close to each other.

Heavenly Father, I pray that Your love eclipses both my anger and my desire to distance myself from my spouse. I pray that we can live near one another so that our child/children can see each of us more frequently. I pray that our daily lives, a gift from You, will be less disrupted due to our separation. Amen.

Prayer to Share a Child/Children in Separation or Divorce

Almighty God, I am ashamed to confess to you that I am so mad at my spouse I do not want to share our child/children. I know this is very wrong. My spouse may have committed grievous wrongs against me, but he/she is a good and loving parent.

God, please help me put away my pettiness. Please help me go the extra mile in this arduous journey. Help us both to be willing to offer the other spouse the right to personally care for a child/children when one of us cannot. Help us both allow our child/children to express and share their pain, wishes, experiences, and concerns without fear of criticism, judgment, or disloyalty to either parent. Amen.

FOUR

Prayers During Divorce

Prayer for God's Presence in Divorce

Almighty God, this is a very dark time for me and my family. I never imagined that our marriage would end in divorce. I pledged to love my spouse until death did us part. We are both alive, but our marriage is dead.

I pray that You will forgive me and my spouse for getting a divorce. I know divorce is wrong in Your Divine eyes. In my daily prayers for forgiveness, support, and direction, please be present for me, my spouse, and our child/children.

Heavenly Father, please do not abandon me in this vale of tears. I pray that Your healing light will illuminate the darkness of divorce and that You will remain with me and those I love always and for evermore. Amen.

Prayer for Preparedness for Divorce

Almighty God, through Your Son Jesus Christ, You let Your children know that we must be prepared to die in Christ in order to have eternal life with You. In Your Son Jesus Christ, we learned that we must be prepared to live in Christ on Earth to truly love and to possess life everlasting.

Heavenly Father, divorce is like the death of everything I hold dear. I feel it is killing me. I pray that You will help me prepare for divorce spiritually, legally, and financially. Please reveal to me that the tragic death of our marriage is an opportunity to learn, love, live, and grow in understanding and participation in your Heavenly Kingdom. Amen.

Prayer to Hire the Attorney Best Suited for Me

Almighty God, when I stood at the altar during our wedding, I never imagined I would one day search for a Christian divorce attorney to represent me.

Heavenly Father, as I interview possible attorneys, please be with me. I need Your wisdom, guidance, and discernment to decide who I should hire. I need more than an attorney who knows the law. Help me find an attorney who has the heart and soul not to cause further injury while my family is in crisis. Protect me from hiring a lawyer, who in the name of zealous advocacy, causes unnecessary expense, conflict, fear, anxiety, or pain to my spouse and our child/children.

I pray to You, Heavenly Father, for courtesy to reign and for love to rule. Please inspire all of us to let olive branches of peace and caring hearts dissolve our marriage, rather than swords or angry threats. May Your Son Jesus Christ, the Prince of Peace, be present with me, my spouse, and the attorneys during every step of the divorce process. Amen.

Prayer to Accept That Divorce is Inevitable

Almighty Father, despite my pleas to drop the divorce proceedings, my spouse refuses. Despite all my prayers and hours of marriage counseling, my spouse refuses to reconcile. I do not want a divorce. However, my lawyer has informed me that the laws of this state allow the court to end our legal relationship as husband and wife, even though I do not condone the divorce.

Heavenly Father, please help me accept this legal outcome and not waste money or recklessly spend the child's/children's college funds fighting legal battles that cannot be won. I place all my hurts, losses, pain, resentment, grief, and anger in Your hands. Only then may I bear the cross of divorce and its consequences with dignity, grace, and strength. Amen.

Prayer for the Most Suitable Divorce Process

Almighty God, my spouse and I must choose the kind of process to be used to resolve our divorce issues. The process we use will affect how much stress, expense, and conflict we will endure in dissolving our marriage.

Heavenly Father, I pray that you help both my spouse and I choose the process most suited to our needs, interests, and goals. May the process we choose not harm our post-divorce relationships with each other, our child/children, or our families. I pray that You will show me the proper path and process to divide our marital property and to lovingly share our child/children. Amen.

Prayer to Find a Suitable Financial Advisor

Almighty God, despite all my efforts to save our marriage, I am a party in a divorce proceeding with my spouse. We have accumulated property that needs to be divided between us.

Heavenly Father, please help me locate a trustworthy Christian financial advisor to gather financial information, to prepare an inventory of our property and to develop settlement options which, if accepted by us, will allow a win-win outcome for both of us. I promise to use my share of our marital property wisely and to the Glory of Your Holy Name. Amen.

Prayer for a Suitable Parenting Planner

Almighty God, in marriage You have blessed us with a child/children. We need guidance on what kind of parenting plan is most suited to our child/children after our divorce. Please lead us to a Christian parenting planner who will help us to establish parenting times and to learn ways to effectively co-parent. Heavenly Father, please provide each of us the best opportunity as parents to nurture, develop, and raise our child/children to be Your servant(s) in the name of Your Son Jesus Christ, Our Lord. Amen.

Prayer for the Best Words to Tell Our Child/Children about the Divorce

Almighty Father, the time has come for us to tell our child/children that we are divorcing. In prayer, please give us the best words to tell our child/children about this difficult decision. As parents, please give us the patience to wait until we can tell the child/children together.

Heavenly Father, please help our child/children understand that the divorce is not something he/she/they caused. Please give us the words to reassure our child/children that the divorce is not his/her/their responsibility to fix or repair. After the divorce, may our child/children live in two separate, happy homes with parents who love them dearly. Let our child/children know that we will never abandon him/her/them, just as You never abandon anyone who truly believes in You. Amen.

Prayer for Uneventful Child Exchanges Between Parents

Almighty God, I confess that when my spouse and I meet to exchange our child/children, we have argued. We have openly criticized the other. We have shown our child/children loud voices and angry faces. I know that this is wrong.

With great sadness, I have come to realize that it harms the child/children more than us when this happens.

Heavenly Father, please help us make all transitions and exchanges of our child/children calm and free of hurtful drama. Support us in not involving our child/children in our problems or parenting issues. I pray that in those moments Your love and peace are present and that all child exchanges are uneventful and full of Your peace, O Lord, Heavenly King of the Peace That Surpasses All Understanding. Amen.

Prayer for Wise Decision-Making

Almighty God, thank You for sending me a very good Christian attorney for my divorce process. However, please help me not be too dependent on my lawyer for everything, so that I may develop my own wisdom to make decisions. To save time and expense, please help me gather and select the optimal team of additional professionals in coaching, parenting, and financial matters to improve the chances of an equitable outcome. If I get the best advice and information, then I can develop and explore all settlement options. Then, I know that I can independently make my own wise decisions. In doubt, I know I can always pray to You for grace and guidance. Amen.

Prayer for Control in Decision-Making in Divorce

Almighty God, through prayer, please lead me to those Christian professionals who will offer me the best information and advice in my divorce. May I never delegate my responsibility for decision-making in the divorce to others, including my attorney, or other family members, or friends.

Heavenly Father, please give me the courage and strength to make all the legal decisions for myself and our child/children. May the difficult decisions be made by me and my spouse, in a loving spirit of mutual concern, when possible, and not be made by the attorneys, the judge, or a jury. Amen.

Prayer to be Treated Fairly in Divorce Despite Wrongdoing

Almighty God, I am responsible for the divorce my spouse has filed against me. My spouse and our child/children have suffered because I have committed wrongs in marriage. I have truly repented. I have asked and continue to ask for Your Divine forgiveness.

Heavenly Father, my spouse is so bitter and angry that I know I am not being treated fairly in the legal process. I pray that my spouse will forgive me and treat me with fairness and understanding. Please help me to stand up for what is fair for both of us as co-parents to our blessed child/children. I know there must be life and love after the divorce. But now, I can only see my spouse's anger, hurt, and resentment. Amen.

Prayer to Avoid Revenge

Almighty God, You have shared and sacrificed Your most precious Son Jesus Christ on the cross so that our lives may be bountiful on Earth and everlasting in Heaven.

I am ashamed that in the settlement of our divorce I want revenge. I want to make my spouse suffer and to pay mightily for divorcing me. I know this is wrong, petty, and selfish.

In prayer, please help me sacrifice my selfishness and pettiness to Your Glory and goodness. Heavenly Father, help me make room in my heart for compassion toward my spouse and his/her needs. Amen.

Prayer to be Healed by God's Grace

Almighty Father, our heartbroken family is suffering terribly amidst the process of divorce. We are standing in the shadow of the Cross waiting to be healed by the Light and Love of the Risen Christ.

Heavenly Father, may we, in prayer, be covered by the blood of Christ, so that what is ill or broken in us is healed. Then, may we be one with You and one in harmony with each other. Amen.

Prayer for a Successful Mediation

Almighty God, as a last-ditch effort to peaceably settle our divorce without a trial, we are going to participate in mediation. Please guide and direct the mediator to lead us to find a resolution which will form a new beginning for each other and for our restructured family.

Heavenly Father, it's hard for me to be in the same room with my spouse. It is almost unbearable to try to dialogue about difficult issues. Please, Almighty God, send us both a spirit of forgiveness, reasonableness, and flexibleness as we endeavor to find solutions to our problems with the assistance of a mediator. Amen.

Prayer for a Favorable Outcome in the Divorce Trial

Almighty God, I have been unable to resolve the divorce issues with my spouse despite prayer, therapy, Christian counseling, and mediation. I want to avoid the stress, harm, and expense of a trial, but my spouse wants to "win" and wants me to "lose" in the divorce. My spouse's energy is focused on blame. I am focused on the future and moving forward in Christ.

Heavenly Father, if it is Your will, may You permit the court to see the truth, ignore the falsehoods, and decide the issues with fairness.

I hold up my faith in You and in Your Heavenly Justice. In that faith, may I accept the outcome from the court of humans. May justice and fairness prevail for both of us in the divorce and for our child/children. Amen.

FIVE

Prayers for After the Divorce

Prayer for a Homemaker Finding a Job

Almighty God, I have spent all the years of my marriage as a dutiful and devoted spouse, homemaker, and parent to our child/children. In doing so, I have sacrificed a career and my own financial independence for the vocation of loving, nurturing, and comforting our child/children and making our home a reflection of Your love, light, and grace.

Heavenly Father, now I must enter the workplace due to divorce. Please support me in this process to find a job which is suited to me and the talents You bestowed upon me at birth. Please remind me that Your Divine Love and kindness exist in all places, including the various locations I may be called upon to earn a living. Amen.

Prayer for Our Restructured Family

Dear Lord, much time has passed since our divorce. My spouse and I now live in separate households. I give thanks to You for supporting me in the post-divorce process and in the monumental changes that have taken place.

Heavenly Father, please help me to see the good things in the life/lives of our child/children in the time they spend with my former spouse. Please open up my heart to hear the joys and experiences they are having at their other home without jealousy or hurt feelings because they are not with me.

Almighty Father, in my time away from our child/children, may I pray and work on my own spiritual growth and relationship with You. With Your Divine guidance, may I learn to more fully love others in Your Holy Name. Amen

Prayer to be Together as Parents at a Child/Children's Celebrations

Almighty God, the court has granted the divorce. Although we are legally divorced, we have a child/children who will always be part of our lives.

Heavenly Father, I pray that you will help me put aside bitterness towards my former spouse so that we all may be together at birthdays, graduations, weddings and other important activities in the life of our child/children without hard feelings or hurtful words and actions toward each other. Amen.

Prayer to Open My Heart Following Divorce

Almighty Father, the court has granted the divorce. The broken marriage, and now the divorce, have shaken my belief in love. I do not know if I will ever be able to open my heart and allow another person to love me again. I doubt that I will ever be capable of loving another person and trusting him/her.

Heavenly Father, as each day passes with my daily prayers to You, may I be less afraid of being vulnerable in love to another human being. Please help me, Dearest Savior, to be more open, not only to Your infinite love, but also to the love and affection of someone who may be a future spouse, if that be Your will. Amen.

SIX

Universal Prayers During Reconciliation/ Separation/Divorce

Prayer for Faith in God

Almighty God, I beg you for the faith in You to sustain me during this painful process. Right now, it is almost impossible for me to see Your Presence shining in the darkness of my spouse's betrayal and the tangle of my confused thoughts.

I pray, Dear Heavenly Father, that you will shore up my faltering faith and remind me that You are the Only One who will never let me down. Amen.

Prayer for Daily Devotion/Time Spent with God

Almighty God, I pray for Your help to remember that the time I spend in prayer with You daily is the best time of my day or night. Time spent with You refreshes me in a way that nothing else can do.

Heavenly Father, please help me to turn to You in my thoughts throughout the day and night. Help me be willing to take time away from my busyness and my complications to simply sit with You and be grateful for all the good that you have already placed in my life. Amen.

Prayer to Overcome Fear of the Unknown Future

Almighty God, I am afraid of losing my spouse, of being away from our children, and of the unknown future. However, I know that we must separate and live apart at this time.

In daily prayer, please give me the courage to follow You into the darkness. I know that even with my eyes closed, if I open my heart in faith and trust in You, You will surely light the path ahead of me. Amen.

Prayer for Daily Exercise

Almighty God, thank you for the body you have given me which is animated with Your precious

Spirit. Please help me to take good care of my body as the temple of the fragile life you have given me. I owe it to You, to myself, and to those who love me and I love, to practice good physical health habits and to exercise often.

Heavenly Father, please assist me in my daily quest to care for my health so that I, as Your Earthly vessel, may be a better and more energetic instrument of Your compassionate love on Earth. Amen.

Prayer to Not be Controlling to My Spouse

Almighty God, I am very anxious and worried at this difficult time. One of the ways that I am dealing with those feelings is to repeatedly call, text, or email my spouse many times during the day when we are not together. She/he understandably claims that I am overly controlling and harassing. In trying to deal with my anxiety in this way, I have learned I am taking actions which undermine the chances of saving the marriage. Regrettably, I am driving away the very spouse with whom I want to spend the rest of my life.

Heavenly Father, during my prayers, please hold my anxious soul in Your hands. Please help me refrain from acting out my anxiety. Instead of pestering and bothering my spouse in these ways, help me to remember that instead, I should just pray to You. You are always looking after my spouse and me, whether we are together or apart.

Please, Dear Heavenly Lord, share with me Your Divine peace which surpasses all understanding. Help me place my trust in You. Amen.

Prayers for Putting Our Child/ Children First

Almighty God, my spouse and I are living separately and need to develop a parenting plan which is best suited to our child/children. Please guide us to develop a plan which puts our child/children first and our needs second.

Heavenly God, please help me to make parenting decisions without bitterness, anger, or hatred towards my spouse. I know that You do not want Your blessed children to be used as pawns by a parent to get back at the other parent. Please help me turn away from the temptation to do so and to turn towards the face of Your Divine Glory, love, and grace. Amen.

Prayer to Shield Children from Marital or Parental Conflict

Almighty God, You have blessed our marriage with a child/children. You have loaned these precious children as gifts to us as parents. We, as parents and as Your servants, are called by You to love, nurture, teach, and instill in every child an abiding faith in You. Unfortunately, our child/children have heard our angry voices and seen our unkind behavior. I fear we have harmed our child/children.

Heavenly Father, please forgive us for exposing our child/children to conflicts between us. I know it takes two people to have an argument. Please help us, as parents, to avoid conflict in front of our child/children. In refraining from arguments and in refraining from venting anger and frustration in front of our child/children, we honor You and show You we truly treasure and love our child/children. Amen.

Prayer to Not Demean My Spouse to a Child

Almighty God, because I have been hurt by my spouse, I am tempted to tell our child/children all the "bad" things my spouse has said or done to me. When I feel like this, I never want to give my spouse the benefit of any doubt, and I always assume the worst about her/him. Please forgive me, Heavenly Father, for succumbing to these temptations.

Great Good God, please help me not speak ill about my spouse. This is very wrong and causes more spiritual injury to our child/children and to me than it will ever cause to my spouse. A child should believe and trust in both parents just as we should always believe and trust in You, the Almighty and Loving Father of all of us. Amen.

Prayer to be a Member of the Blood and Body of Christ

Almighty God, I know You are present with me when I pray. As a member of the Church and the Body of Christ's work on Earth, I need to be in Your Heavenly Presence too. My words, thoughts, and deeds, in communion with others, should reflect Your Divine love.

Heavenly Father, I pray that You help me reflect and share Your love with my spouse and our child/children at this difficult time. Later, please help me to understand, to forgive, and to show kindness, compassion and mercy to the one who has broken my heart, who has been untrustworthy, and/or suffered from an addiction. Please open my heart to wish that my spouse obtain the best outcome possible in our divorce, so that my spouse may be able to do the same for me. I ask this in the name of Your Precious Son, Our Lord Jesus Christ. Amen.

Prayer for the Lord's Safe Harbor

Almighty God, I am secure with my faith and trust in You completely. Wherever this unwanted journey in separation takes me, may I be calm and trustful in the safe harbor of Your love for me.

Great Heavenly Father, my life on Earth and my faith in eternal love and life in Heaven are both anchored in You and Your Son Jesus Christ.

Wherever I go, You are always with me. Thank you, Almighty God, for this and for all Your Gracious Heavenly blessings that You have poured into the cup of my earthly life. Amen.

SEVEN

My Prayers for God's Help

Prayerful Passages is a **Bending Angel Project**. All these works are born from the inspiration received by author Jack H. Emmott from a painting he purchased at a charity art show in the 1990s. This painting of a Bending Angel was created by renowned Texas Artist of the Year, the late Charles Schorre.

The mission of **Bending Angel Projects** is to invite Christians through prayer, story, poetry and art to more fully experience the love and presence of God and His Angels.

Coming soon is the book *Bending Angel* also written by Jack H. Emmott. In *Bending Angel* the author shares stories of the angels who have delivered God's messages of love, light, hope, and healing as the author struggled with the devastation and darkness of polio. *Bending Angel* invites the reader to watch for his/her own angels. Those angels that the author believes appear here and now, and are not only in the biblical past. Look for the publication date at <u>www.Bendingangel.com</u>.

CPSIA information can be obtained at www.ICGtesting.com
Printed in the USA
BVOW05s2225180216

437272BV00012B/78/P